ALL THE THINGS A GIRL CAN BE

Copyright © 2019 by Tanner Tate
All rights reserved. This book or any portion thereof may not be reproduced or used in any manner whatsoever without the express written permission of the publisher except for the use of brief quotations in a book review.

Printed in the United States of America

First Printing, 2019

ISBN 978-0-578-61631-5

DadBeard Publishing
629 Old English Rd.
Edmond, OK 73003

To my favorite, Lorelai.

All The Things A Girl Can Be

by **Tanner Tate**

illustrated by **Morgan Snyder**

The world is full of people being all the things you see.

That means billions of people have billions of things to be.

So never feel less than equal because there's nothing girls can't be.

You can be AMBITIOUS.

Like an entrepreneur.

You can be
STRONG.

Like a builder.

You can be CONFIDENT.

Process of SAVING $1,000,000.⁰⁰ starts today!!

How to INVEST

Like an investor.

You can be all of these things and so much more, you see.

Because all of the things are things a girl can be.

www.ingramcontent.com/pod-product-compliance
Lightning Source LLC
Chambersburg PA
CBHW040732150426
42811CB00063B/1585